Through the 'I' of the soul

Salv Ridino

Table of contents

Keywords:

Supernatural agency, Subjective experience, Cognitive

Science of Religion (CSR),

God, Soul, Self,

Christians, Atheists, Gnostics

Abstract

Much literature in the cognitive science of religion (CSR) field suggests that the subjective experience of God is not considered as relevant to explain the belief in supernatural agency. Instead, my personal experience suggests that subjective experience is key to the understanding of such a phenomenon. Therefore, this study aims to fill the gap in the literature of CSR by exploring how the subjective experience of God is understood amongst three different groups, namely: Christians, atheists, and Gnostics. A sample of seven participants per each group was purposefully recruited across different locations in England. Participants were individually interviewed and a thematic analysis, with a slant of Interpretative Phenomenological Analysis (IPA), was employed to draw similarities and differences among the interviewees. Psychological phenomena such as: self, agency, intersubjectivity, and ontological categories were found to be relevant to the subjective experience of God. Surprisingly, findings also showed that the differences between categories of belief can be fuzzy.

Introduction and Background

Cognitive scientists of religion (CSR's) advocate that the explanation for supernatural agent belief is to be found within the cognitive processes of the human mind. Conversely, my personal experience suggests that there is more than just cognitive processes involved in the formulation and belief that these entities exist.

Supernatural agents (Pyysiäinen, 2009) like gods, are representations of non-human agents that employ the same cognitive mechanisms that we use to represent ourselves and fellow human beings. The belief (Barrett, 2004) in supernatural agents is produced by natural mental processes that occur in ordinary environments. However, as a process, it (Boyer, 2001) depends upon a series of cognitive mechanisms that serve other specific functions in the mind of the individual. Furthermore, supernatural agents like gods (Barrett and Keil, 1996) are understood as essentially defying all ontological categories; the fundamental distinction between all the different existing things. The defiance of these distinctions is a necessary characteristic (Boyer, 2000) that, within certain degrees of plausibility, enables concepts of supernatural entities to spread through the cognitive system of the wider population.

However, the CSR literature perused for this report was lacking reference to the subjective experience of the human individual in the formation of supernatural agency concepts and consequent belief. The term subjective experience (Harris, 2014) can be understood as the feeling of having a self within us that undergoes or gets directly involved in an event. This aspect (Boyer, 2001) of human experience seems to have been discarded as not yielding useful information to understand the cerebral structures of religion. Nonetheless, my personal experience suggests that there is more than just cognitive explanations to the issue of supernatural agency. Notably, the unwavering certainty (Hart, 2013) that each and every person has of their own subjective experience constitutes the bedrock of all religious and non-religious beliefs. If a Christian believer claims that they are experiencing the presence or even a relationship with God, it should be enough to recognize that these people are having an experience that is real, at least to them (Harris, 2014). The same should apply to people whose subjective experience diverge from that of Christians. Atheists (Dawkins, 2006) and Gnostics (Hoeller, 2002), for example, have different

8

approaches to supernatural agency. Indeed, subjective experience is an essential component of cognition that deserves more attention in pursuing the reasons of belief and disbelief.

Therefore, by conducting interviews with Christians, Gnostics, and atheists, I aim to produce an analysis that could help answer the following Research Question (RQ):

How do Christians, Gnostics, and atheists make meaning of their subjective experience of God?

Literature Review

The idea of God

An issue presented by the CSR's is about their concern over ontological categories of supernatural agents, and in particular of God (Barrett, 2004). Their argument is that supernatural agents should necessarily comprise a mix of naturalistic and non-naturalistic characteristics. Barrett and Keil (1996) use the term non-naturalistic to emphasize the theological claim that God is of a different type of being than humans. Immateriality is a non-naturalistic characteristics attributed to God. Furthermore, Boyer (1994) argues that if supernatural agents did not violate ontological categories up to a certain degree, their idea would die out. However, the supernatural agent idea should not be too counterintuitive either, lest it would have the same fate. Hence, the combination of anthropomorphic features with non-naturalistic attributes.

Conversely, Hart (2013) explains that the definition of God violates, or better transcends, all sorts of ontological categories. Consequently, saying that God is everywhere naturally fosters riddles where "within" is the same as "without". God, for Hart, is by definition boundless, and omnipresent. It is not a being in the sense of possessing discreteness and finiteness, just like other objects. Nonetheless, it can dispense and take existence away from objects. Indeed, objects are usually understood as existing in space and time, and their being and existence as dependent upon the universe. Whereas the common description of the feeling of God, the Christian God, is that it is the only one who can be understood, and intimately perceived, as transcending as well as encompassing every existing objects at the same time. This brings about the idea of God as a holistic entity; bigger than the sum of its parts (Aristotle, 1957). Therefore, while CSR's try to assign God into an ontological category, believers may hold different views on the nature of being of God; all depending from their own subjective experience.

The Subjective Experience of the self

The individual's (Harris, 2014) subjective experience is based upon the idea of self. This idea aims to illustrate the individual's sense of being the subject of experience; the "cause in esse" (Hart,

2013), or "cause in being", explained as the essence of the individual.

Indeed, according to Leary and Buttermore (2003), the self delineates the possibility to consider oneself as the object of one's own attention. Neisser (1988) identified five kinds of self-knowledge: ecological, interpersonal, extended, private, and conceptual. Specifically, the private and the conceptual self-knowledge are relevant to this study. The private self (Leary and Buttermore, 2003) is the ability to elaborate subjective information such as feelings and intentions that cannot be accessed by others. This ability enables to reduce the sense of separateness and to overcome the limits imposed by the private self (Leary and Buttermore, 2003). The conceptual self, also referred to as symbolic self, is the ability to represent one's own experience in abstract and symbolic ways. Thus, self-representations and self-concepts are generally talked about through a system of traits, labels, and categories that people use to mentally visualise the content of their subjective experience.

The idea of the self, Smart (1996) observed, has been associated with the idea of the soul of many ancient traditions. By the word 'soul' (Collins Dictionary) it is meant the part of an individual that entails their mind and personality. Tylor (1958) referred to the soul as an important element in the origins of religion and coined the term animism to indicate the belief that anything has got a life force within. Also, Spencer (1876) argued that the origins of religion are to be sought in the observation that the soul can transcend the limits of the physical body.

Unfortunately, there seems to be very little literature about the concept of soul in the CSR field. Only Pyysiäinen (2009) dedicates some space to the concept. Indeed, when attempting to explain the reasons why the belief in supernatural agency is so widespread across the globe and history, prominent researchers like Boyer (2001) and Barrett (2004) hardly mention the concept of soul, if they do it. They do refer to spirits. Yet, they refer to them as entities that are treated as external to the individual believer. Instead, Pyysiäinen (2009) draws a distinction between the religious conceptualisation of the soul and the sense of the individual that they have a soul, or self, occupying and animating their bodies.

Agency

Pyysiäinen (2009), besides recognising that the concept of soul and that of self are folk psychological representations that attempt to explain human agency, also demonstrates that the concept of agency is, indeed, the cornerstone of supernatural agency representations. In this regard, Barrett (2004) postulates the existence of a cognitive mechanism, the HADD (Hyperactive Agent Detection Device), that would activate every time there is the need to identify an agent behind an event. This device is also characterised by its hyperactive functionality which can get triggered by small stimuli. In an evolutionary context, this would allow our ancestors to spot, for example in the brush of a forest, a potential life threatening enemy. On the downside, CSR's (Barrett, 2004) argue that the eagerness of this device to spot agency also for events that have seemingly no agent behind them, like leaves rustling in the wind,

may be the trigger that leads people to believe in supernatural agency.

Behind the idea of this cognitive device, however, there seems to be the assumption that the belief in supernatural agency originated by observing, and not being able to explain, external events. Indeed, this device does not account for those inner events where the sense of self-agency plays a role. Self-agency is the sense and ability of an individual to recognise that they have been the author of their actions (Jeannerod, 2003), and it (Voyer and Franks, 2014) can be sensed along three different modalities: implicit, intermediate, and explicit. The implicit modality, opposite to the explicit one, refers to the lack of information about the action; the individual does not know what the action might be, and why they have performed it, although they are still able to assign their own authorship to it.

However, people (Harris, 2014) spontaneously attribute their own agency, implicit or otherwise, to the self, as if the self were a "homunculus" occupying their bodies and having conscious intention and purpose to perform actions. This is the sense of 'I' that authors behavioural and cognitive actions such as hearing, talking and thinking. The 'I', therefore, besides being the "cause in esse", the essence of the individual, contains also the sense (Hart, 2013) of becoming; the "cause in fiery", or "cause in becoming". This sense is generally experienced as the inner force that puts us in relation with other things and entities.

Intersubjectivity

The relation between two or more subjects is known as intersubjectivity (Reich, 2010). Intersubjectivity is based on the natural tendency of human beings to mind-read others and feel to be mind-read by others (Gergely and Csibra, 2003). However, also supernatural agents are conceptualised as being able to be mind-reading and mind-read (Pyysiäinen, 2009). Barrett (2008) assigns two main features to supernatural agents: animacy and mentality. The ability to attribute mentality is called Theory of Mind (ToM) (Nichols and Stich, 2003). This ability enables the individual to attribute conscious intention to another agent. Pyysiäinen (2009) argues that when an individual assigns an invisible agent to an event whose causes are not directly intelligible, a process of hyperactive understanding of intentionality (HUI) comes in place. This mechanism supports the tendency to assign mentality to an invisible agent for events that are seemingly without a plausible cause. The HUI, like the HADD, accounts for external supernatural entities.

Indeed, similarly to the HADD, the HUI does not account for the attribution of intentionality that the individual does to their self, or soul. Nichols (2000) explains, the individual's attribution of mentality to oneself may be the outcome of the ToM used to reflect on one's own states of mind. In this sense, the concept of intersubjectivity (Auerbach, 1998) can be applied to the inner interaction between the two aspects of the self; I-me (Mead, 1934, 2015). Mead postulated that the essence of the self is in the continuous interaction between the subject 'I' and the object 'me'; where the 'I' is the observer, and the 'me' is the object of observations. Therefore, while the HUI model may account for the intentionality ascribed to God understood as an external entity, it does not account for the intentionality the individual assigns to their inner self.

Categories of belief

Generally speaking, Christians, Gnostics, and atheists have different approaches to supernatural agency and, specifically, to God .

Christians

Christian (BBC) people believe there is just one God who is perfect, omnipotent, omnipresent, and omniscient; whose son, Jesus Christ, resurrected after being killed on the cross. Although Christians are divided amongst several strands and different views, all Christians claim that they communicate with God by the means of prayer. Prayer, as well as worship, love, and mystical experiences are the ways whereby humans can get to know God. Also, (Geden, 1922) believing in the immortality of the soul, which they define as immaterial and immortal: Christians claim that when the body dies, the soul loses its earthily personality and gets absorbed by God. Christians' belief (Keller, 2008) in God is usually backed up by the claim that there must be a contingent cause behind the natural creation of existence, and keeps intervening in its existence.

A survey conducted by the Pew Research Center (2011) in 2010 estimated over 2 billion Christians around the world, making Christianity the largest religion in the world.

Atheists

In neat opposition to Christian belief, atheists (Collins Dictionary) reject the belief that there is any god. Gray (2018) suggests that atheists are those who make no use of the idea of God when pondering about creation. In fact, atheists consider science and reason (Hitchens, 2007), although not sufficient, as necessary factors. On this basis, they (Dawkins, 2006) assert that there is not enough evidence for the existence of God; neither as the source of the universe, nor as the personal presence professed by many.

Also atheists, however, are of many types (Gray, 2018). In his spectrum of probabilities, Dawkins (2006) shows that the difference between atheists goes from agnostics who lean towards atheism, to strong atheists who can confidently claim that they "know there is no god".

Unfortunately, because of the scarce agreement on the meaning of atheism, no reliable data is available to gauge their population. In the Pew Research Center survey (2012), atheists were included in the 18% of those who declared not to have a religious affiliation. However, having no religious affiliation does not amount to being atheist. In fact, this percentage includes, amongst others, atheists and agnostics, as well as people who are somewhat spiritual and believe in the existence of God.

Gnostics

Gnostics are part of the invisible category of people who identify themselves as having no religious affiliation, although they may declare themselves as spiritual and surely accepting the existence of God as real. Jung (1875-1961), considered an authoritative reference for Gnostics (Hoeller, 1982), once said that he *knew* about the existence of God, rather than just believing. Indeed, Gnostics (Pagels, 1979) centre their perspective on God in the direct knowledge achievable only through the subjective experience of the individual; gnosis. Conversely to Christians, it (Hoeller, 2002) is through their inner self that the individual can transcend the earthly reality and unite with God, perceived as the ultimate reality.

In the Western world, Gnosticism (Gray, 2018) is mainly associated with Christianity –Christian Gnosticism- as the mystical side of the official institution of the Church. It has developed in many different strands. It is nowadays acknowledged that Gnostics ideas are present in many religious and philosophical traditions, thus having different names like Sufism, and have, in time, developed new forms like the Universal Gnosticism of Samael Aon Weor (1917-1977).

Rationale

Christians, atheists, and Gnostics seem, at least apparently, to approach the idea of God from different perspectives, very likely building on their own individual subjective experience. Nonetheless, there is little discussion in the CSR field regarding psychological phenomena relevant to the experience of God from a subjective perspective. These phenomena are: soul, agency, intersubjectivity, and transcendence. Hence, this study aims to contribute to fill this gap in the CSR literature by seeking an answer to the following research question:

How do Christians, Gnostics, and atheists make meaning of their subjective experience of God?

Methodology

Research design

In this study, I used a qualitative research design (Mayan, 2009) in order to capture and understand the meaning Christians, atheists, and Gnostics make of their subjective experiences of the idea of God.

Situating the researcher

My Christian upbringing, atheist teenage background, and current interests in Gnosticism, is at the basis of my decision to interview people from these three different groups. Also, this background provided me with the relevant confidence to delve into the different understandings of God and attempt an interpretation of the phenomenon from the three different perspectives. None of my participants had the full picture of my 'religious experience' prior to the interview. Some of my participants became aware of my background only during the debriefing session. This allowed me to ask them questions as if I were completely ignorant on certain aspects of their beliefs. At the same time, I was able to show them empathy when they were struggling for words that could best describe their experience. Also, my personal experience made me notice that the literature of CSR does not discuss the subjective experience of the individual. All this motivated me to seek evidence from direct sources that could contribute to the debate and help bridge the gap in the literature.

Instruments

I conducted semi-structured individual interviews which allowed unanticipated ideas and opinions to emerge and be further explored when deemed relevant to my RQ (UK Data Service, 2018a). More importantly, semi-structured interviews (Bauer and Gaskell, 2008) helped to capture personal and unique understandings of, and attitudes towards, the idea of God. They (Fylan, 2005) enabled participants to converse openly about their personal views on God, and flexibly when they, or I, felt the need to expand on their concepts and insights. A topic guide (Bauer and Gaskell, 2008) was prepared in advance to help me keep the focus on the relevant issues to discuss within the set time. However, the original topic guide had to undergo two different amendments along the study. The first time, after the third interview, I amended and dropped a few questions. This was done mainly in virtue of time constraints, or for the leading assumptions embedded in some of the questions. The second time, after the tenth interview, I amended or dropped other questions where entities different from God were mentioned; namely, angels and demons. This time, the amendments were mainly driven by the fact that most participants seemed more inclined to talk about God than other entities.

Sampling

The sample consisted of 21 people evenly distributed across the three different categories of belief (7x Christians, 7x atheists, 7x Gnostics). Participants are, at times, generically referred to as Christians, Gnostics, and atheists in this report. I only use these terms to refer to my participants. Their age ranged from 23 to 66 (average age: 39). I purposefully recruited every participant (Mayan, 2009), as it was important to select individuals whose religious identity and will to talk about their subjective experience fitted the aim of my research.

Several groups, churches, and associations were also contacted. Two Christian churches, two atheist associations, and one Gnostic group did not want to get involved, or did not respond. Particular difficulties were encountered in recruiting Gnostics, in the sense that it was hard to access them. Thirteen participants were acquaintances with whom I had conversed about the general topic of religion in the past. Two participants introduced me to others who were willing to participate in my study. Whilst four Christians and five Gnostics were part of groups and churches, no atheist declared any affiliation to any particular atheist association. Interviews took place, face-to-face, in various locations around London; except two of them which were conducted over the phone, due to the inability to meet in person with the participants who did not live in London. Their gender was a random mix of females and males and not relevant to the purpose of this study.

Procedure

Full ethical approval was given to the research by the Ethics Board of the LSE department of Psychological and Behavioural Science. No "ethically important moments" (Guillemin and Gillam, 2004) were either anticipated or happened. Participants were fully briefed and where concerns were raised these were discussed and clarified before their interview started. All participants gave written consent (UK Data Service, 2018b), except one whose full consent was verbally recorded, over the phone, prior to the interview taking place. Interviews took place in different settings: from rooms around the LSE campus, to parks nearby participants' locations. In every case, the location was chosen in agreement with the participants in order for them to feel comfortable (Bauer and Gaskell, 2008). The length of the interviews ranged from 25 to 95 minutes (Average length = 43 minutes). After every interview, I debriefed my participants as an opportunity to answer their questions, if any. All participants were provided with contact information in case any concern would arise. All participants (Fujii, 2012) were given a pseudonym in order to anonymize their identity.

Methods of analysis

I audio-recorded all the interviews and verbatim transcribed them. After familiarising myself with the content of the interviews (Rice and Ezzy, 1999), I used a thematic analysis (Braun and Clarke, 2006) with a slant of IPA (Pietkiewicz & Smith, 2014). A particular focus was given to statements pointing to emotions, ideas, and insights. Codes (Boyatzis, 1998) were identified as inductively emerging from the texts of the interviews. There were no theory-induced codes. Codes were collated in a codebook, reviewed for relevance towards the RQ, and grouped into themes (Feredey and Cochrane, 2006) ensuring that thematic meanings did not overlap. There was sufficient ground to use similar coding for all interviews, as all codes emerged in very similar patterns across the three categories of participants. An average of 85% inter-code reliability was established over four interviews. No software was used.

Analysis

The analysis produced 27 codes which were grouped into 15 categories. These 15 categories were grouped into five major themes; namely: 'The idea of God', 'Soul', 'Agency', 'Intersubjectivity', and 'Categories of belief'. These themes will be presented in details in this section. The themes report participants' subjective experience in relation to the different aspects that characterise their belief, or non-belief, in God. While the last theme, 'Categories of belief', is being chosen to highlight a surprise encountered during the analysis of the interviews, the first four themes are strictly relevant to the RQ:

How do Christians, Gnostics, and atheists make meaning of their subjective experience of God?

The idea of God

This theme aims to convey the idea that participants have of God as an entity that eludes the anthropomorphic descriptions used to talk about it. In fact, it locates within the CSR debate on the ontological categories assigned to God (Barrett and Keil, 1996).

Omnipresence

Emma, a Christian girl, concisely described her idea of God as an omnipresence that, at the same time, is unique and all-knowledgeable:

He is the one. He is just everything. He knows everything. He's the alpha. – Emma, Christian

Gnostics associated God with the idea of an all-pervading and all-embracing consciousness, not just belonging to the single individual. However, their idea of consciousness did not differ much from the Christian idea of God. James talked of consciousness in these terms:

But I think the only thing that is actually anywhere is consciousness. And God is the whole thing. So God is consciousness, not just your own little window onto it, but the whole thing. – James, Gnostic

The idea of an all-pervading God brings Gnostics to affirm that every living and not living thing is God themselves. Jacob enthusiastically declared:

You are God! And I am God. And so he, she, every living and not living thing. – Jacob, Gnostic

This idea that God is in everything, as well as in humans, was shared by Christians; although they used milder words when pronouncing it, as Chloe did:

So actually by already saying that God is all around you, you're already saying that God can be anything. It's just always there, in the air you're breathing, in the molecules that make up a table. It could be anything. And God can take any shape or form. – Chloe, Christian

Gnostics explained that the universe is made of energy which takes different forms; one of these forms is matter. Daniel said:

I understand the universe of being formed entirely of energy, here in the physical world crystallised into matter. – Daniel, Gnostic

31

Only few atheists touched upon this theme. Those who did, like Ely, would agree with Christians and Gnostics. God is just everywhere:

Everywhere. Not in a specific place. Even if I think maybe in the universe, I can't think of a place. – Ely, Atheist

Linking oneness

The omnipresence of God leads to the idea that the whole is somewhat organically organised and pervading; all is in oneness. The current theme aims to convey the way participants discussed the idea of a holistic sense of reality. Gnostics associated the idea of God to such a feeling. Following the logic that God is everything, Gnostics explained that God is not just one single entity, whereas it is a combination of many entities. In the words of Gabriel:

God is a multiple unity. It is not one entity it is a combination of many entities and that God has unfolded itself in all the different aspects of the

universe which were created, and were part of.
— Gabriel, Gnostic

From an atheistic standpoint, Hazel wondered why there should be just one God and not as many as there are individuals on the earth. In a sort of Gnostic embryo, her idea was expressed this way:

And I also think why there would necessarily be one god or one power, because there are millions of human beings. So surely if there was another type of being, some sort of god, deity, or whatever, there wouldn't necessarily be just one. — Hazel, Atheist

Four atheists shared the feeling that the individual is part of a bigger reality organically organised. Ely talked of a network that transcends physicality and connects all human beings:

The entity that I'm thinking about is more to do with super intelligence that links human beings together and enables them to connect in a way that is not just physical. — Ely, atheist

Ely's words were echoed by Mike's feeling that there must be something enveloping people, whether they are conscious or not:

There must be something that collectively is seeking us, is around us all the time, even if we are not aware. – Mike, atheist

In their turn, Mike's idea resonated with Gnostics as well. David averred:

In God there is no me, we are all one. – David, Gnostic

Penny described this sense of being part of just one thing as oneness, and added that there would be times when this sense could be disrupted, by anxiety for example:

Yeah, it's like a feeling of oneness. In those moments [of anxiety] I would be disconnected from things. – Penny, atheist

Whereas Hazel, Jack, and John simply disagreed. Hazel said to have no confidence in the idea of being part of a bigger scheme of things that unite under the same entity or force. Things appear to be disconnected from one another, for her:

> *From lack of being convinced otherwise that there is a bigger ultimate power that is all knowing, all influencing, all powerful. Because everything seems too disjointed for that. – Hazel, atheist*

To further dismantle the idea of a virtual network connecting all humans under the same one thing are the words of John, who humbly said that his links are just with his friends, nothing beyond that:

> *I have links with my friends, really. But anything beyond that, no. – John, atheist*

Whilst atheists showed to be quite concerned with this issue, Christians did not raise the theme of reality as a whole unity, or otherwise.

Part of a bigger scheme

Although not making references to a big enveloping unity, Christians still believed that we are part of a bigger scheme, and the bigger scheme being God. Amelie, a Christian girl, exposed it this way:

I believe our soul is connected with God because through our soul we can love God. – Amelie, Christian

The soul was contextualised as being part of a network, for as small as it could be a circle of friends. Christians and Gnostics spoke of the soul as connected with the holistic reality of God. Gnostics spoke of the soul as an entity that is part of a bigger entity. David, for example, hinted to the idea that the individual's soul is a fraction of God:

Soul maybe is a part of full God. – David, Gnostic

Atheists like Hazel, Jack, and John rejected the idea of an ultimate reality capable of joining everybody from within. Whereas other atheists described the relationship between the whole and the individual as capable of taking the features of a big flow and a vessel whose purpose is to be filled. Penny, for example, described this feeling with these words:

I always think it feels not really me, like it comes from somewhere higher up and I'm sort of like a vessel for some sort of higher creative flow that's happening. – Penny, atheist

Even those atheists like Ely who accepted the idea of the soul as an intrinsic quality of the individual, saw it as an enabling medium of a network that lets certain people feel closer to certain others:

Because I do think that we have souls that maybe allow you to feel closer to a person than you would to another. – Ely, atheist

Soul

This theme builds upon the participants' discussion over their sense of self and understanding of the concept of soul. Similarities across the three groups were found in relation to their subjective experience of self. All Christians referred to this concept as that of soul. Similarly, all Gnostics but one; James. He made references to self, rather than soul. Four atheists rejected the idea of soul and rather preferred to refer to the concept of self. Considering the importance that participants gave to the soul, and that the same concept has not been discussed at length in CSR (Pyysiäinen, 2009), a more in depth discussion on the subject should be conducted.

The essential being

The soul was understood as the sense of being and awareness amongst Christians:

It's your sense of awareness, your sense of being. – Chloe, Christian

Also, it was the opinion of Gnostics that the soul is the sense of being (*essence*) that outlives the human body after its death. Jacob explained that the soul is the only thing that transcends physicality:

It is my suspicion that death is not the end. One thing we sort of know is that we don't take our physicality with us. So if there is some essence that goes with us, then that's where I would be looking – Jacob, Gnostic

Christians made no reference during our interviews to the exact course of the soul after life. Yet, similarly to Gnostics, Christians agreed that the soul is the eternal essence of the individual. Concisely, Oliver exposed his view:

It's an everlasting thing and the inner essence that makes you you. – Oliver, Christian

Echoing Oliver's words and pointing out that the soul functions as some sort of compass in life, Rose added:

The soul is the thing that is meant to last forever. It's everlasting so when you die your

soul continues to the afterlife. It's not a tangible thing that you can hold on to. I think if it does exist, it informs the way how you act and what you do to some degree. – Rose, Christian

Jack is one of the four atheists who rejected the idea of soul. Yet, as the other three atheists, he referred to the idea of self and, specifically, to that of psyche:

Do I believe in a person's soul? No! My psyche is in charge of my dreams. It's my history that creates, it's my knowledge, it's my expectations, my fears, my will, my wishes. – Jack, atheist

This link between soul and self was backed up by Hazel who saw the concept of soul as an explanation for the individual's physical and psychological phenomena that have yet to be fully explained:

We don't know enough about the human body to make sense of all our feelings and emotions and behaviours. The soul is an explanation for something that hasn't just been worked out yet. – Hazel, atheist

Representation of consciousness

Besides the idea that the soul can be the set of feelings and emotions held by the individual, some atheists like Penny regarded the soul as the individual's consciousness and their inner voice:

Like the thing that is inside you that is kind of like your consciousness. Like the voice in your head kind of talking to you. – Penny, atheist

The idea of soul representing the individual's consciousness was widely shared by all Gnostics. In the words of Dylan:

The soul is the consciousness of the person. – Dylan, Gnostic

When Gnostics described what happens to the soul when the body dies. Apparently, the soul is not *clean* when dwelling in the body; the ego is attached to it. Dylan summarised this view as follows:

When your soul leaves your body, it will go back into the consciousness but at that time you will lose your ego, you will lose your personality, you're no longer 'Joe Blogg'; you will just be a clean soul. – Dylan, Gnostic

Four atheists made reference to the poor scientific understanding of the soul, and John summarised it this way:

Science can't answer. Consciousness, soul, unconsciousness, thought, whatever, that's an area we probably, if we ever want to understand it, probably we're hundreds of years away from doing it. – John, atheist

Agency

All participants rejected the idea that God can determine their life. They all emphasised their agency and free will. Strictly related to the idea of soul, or self, participants discussed the idea of agency. The main debate in CSR (Barrett, 2004) about agency is whether there is a specific cognitive mechanism that leads believers to attribute agency to a supernatural entity when the causes of an event are unknown.

Supernatural agency

All participants expressed their feeling that God does not exercise agency onto them. Chloe explained:

I don't think that God really intervenes in anything really. – Chloe, Christian

However, God can exercise influence over the individual believer, as Emma told me:

I went to a Catholic retreat and everyone was praying, everyone singing, and I felt a moment I was close to God. When I feel I'm close to God, and I'm having a moment, I will cry my eyes out. And [that time] I couldn't stop crying even though I didn't feel like. I felt that God was with me. We were close. – Emma, Christian

Yet, all atheists thought that believing in God equals believing in predetermined behaviours and actions deliberately prompted by God. On this

43

ground, Penny deemed deplorable the belief that God is responsible for one's own action as a way to avoid one's own responsibility. With reproach, Penny pointed out:

I just think it's passing the buck. You're not owning your own destiny. Which I think you should. – Penny, atheist

While they did not conceive of their actions as predetermined by any supernatural agent, Christians still saw themselves as being at the service of God. Amelie said:

It's my role to know and understand my position and influence in my community and in life and to walk in that in order to be a positive instrument of God. – Amelie, Christian

Self-agency

All participants, however, spoke of their sense of agency as independent from God. Oliver summarised the feeling this way:

I have agency, I don't think that God's gonna decide what happens if I don't do my work, God's not gonna go and magically fix it. – Oliver, Christian

Atheists would happily echo this sense of independent agency from God:

It's always me performing the task. I'm always in charge. I'm responsible for what I do. I'm responsible for what I think. It's always me performing anything that I do. - Jack, atheist

Gnostics, instead, associated their sense of conscious and deliberate agency to a sense of supernatural agency. Daniel encapsulated this feeling in these words:

If we have 100% control of our divine soul we become a master or an angel and then we would say we have free will. – Daniel, Gnostic

Intersubjectivity

My private self

All Christians saw their relationship with God as a means to escape from the distinctiveness of their private self that separates them from other fellow humans. Nobody can ever understand another person as God does. Not even oneself is capable of making sense of one's own aspects as much as God can. This was outlined by Eve as follows:

Because I can show people so much of me they can only get so much of me. They would never get fully all of me, if that makes sense. But because I see that I was created by God, God knows me, God understands me in my entirety in all aspects of myself in ways that I don't even understand myself. – Eve, Christian

The sense of the individual of not being able to share their deep, inner feelings and meanings with others is often understood as an existential issue. This brings to mind the idea of the private self as explicated by Leary and Buttermore (2003). Participants expressly confessed of finding relief in the sense they have of being mind-read by God. Atheists like Penny expressed this concern and understanding for why Christians believe in God:

I don't think you ever really gonna be able to understand someone else's mind even if you are super close to them. He's still a different person to you. I get why it would be comforting to have a God or believe in something that is bigger than you, that you don't have to worry. – Penny, atheist

This is confirmed by Christians who, in fact, attributed to God the ability to know their mind that no one else has. Isabel said:

No one can see what's going on inside me, only God. – Isabel, Christian

God's mind

However, participants also spoke of their ability to infer about God's mind. In the words of Oliver, all Christians alluded to a God's purpose to be found in creation:

But God created it with his own purposes in mind – Oliver, Christian

Gnostics, through the beautiful words of Stella, explained that to understand God you have to feel it within:

We have to look within to feel it. It's like 'where do you locate beauty?' Beauty you see it, you feel it through a connection, first. Depending on your inner state. – Stella, Gnostic

To further explain the concept of connection with God, Gabriel explained that God's mind can be intelligible if the individual tunes into the right frequencies of consciousness:

The only way to understand the mind of God or the divine Mother would be through the different levels of consciousness. So we have to get in a state tuned into the right frequency. – Gabriel, Gnostic

Atheists made no reference to the possibility of knowing God's mind.

I-God

The sense of connection that the believer has with supernatural entities is mainly explicated as communication between the devotee and God. This theme (Boyer, 2001) catches on the issue of rituals like prayers where people talk to statues or themselves. Although a bit abrupt, Jack best summarised the feelings of another three atheists in regards to praying:

I don't know why people pray, I don't understand it. I think it's a waste of time. - Jack, atheist

Christians responded to this claim by explaining that there is a real sense of communication between them and God. As Oliver noted:

There's a real sense of being able to ask questions and get answers back. I genuinely believe I get answers. – Oliver, Christian

Indeed, Christians described a sense of relationship with God that resembles a human relationship. As Emma pointed out:

A relationship with Jesus is when you have a connection with him that you can talk to him. You don't feel you have to be rigid like you don't need to be on your knees praying. I can be sitting down and praying to God and talk to him like an everyday person. – Emma, Christian

Assuming that the talking the Christians refer to could be a physical talking, three atheists concluded that hearing the 'physical' voice of an invisible entity could only be the effect of a brain malfunction. In a half-funny, half-concerned way, John put it this way:

If someone starts seeing angels or hearing voices, I would assume that something is misfiring in their brain. – John, atheist

By making it clear that it is only a metaphorical way of expressing their sense of communication with God, Christians also expressed that sensation that such relationship is obviously a special relationship. Eve said:

I think that the relationship goes beyond a normal relationship in the sense that obviously it's not somebody talking back to you. – Eve, Christian

All Gnostics shared the same feeling as Christians that there can be a connection with God. By referring to divine forces, rather than God specifically, they explained that this connection can be jeopardised by the material world. This is what Gnostics sustained in relation to the sense of connection between the individual and God, and the individual and their inner divine forces. Daniel explained that:

Normally these divine forces whether they're internal or external can't communicate with us because our attention is always on the physical world and not opened to that communication. – Daniel, Gnostic

Christians discussed the same issue. It is possible to connect with God through channels that are not bogged down by the physicality of the day to day routines. Dreams, which are a subconscious manifestation of the psychology of people, are indicated as possible channels of communication. Emma pointed out that:

God can talk to you through dreams. – Emma, Christian

Three atheists accepted the idea of praying and meditation as ways to make people feel closer to God, like Hazel guessed:

I guess with prayer and meditation the idea is that makes you as a person more peaceful, but actually it brings you more closely, or makes you connect more with this God or this higher being. – Hazel, atheist

I-me

Participants also spoke of a dialogue taking place within the individual. A Gnostic participant, Jacob, presented this inner dialogue as a chatter that would stop when turning his attention to it. Also, Jacob discussed the occasional feeling of an inner voice giving him nice and short tips:

When I go into it, the chatter stops. The internal dialogues stop. The inner voice speaks in hardly any voice at all. Really like 2, 3 or 4

*words you'll hear. These things like "go left",
things like "enjoy yourself" or "be free". Tiny
things, sometimes it feels like clichés. – Jacob,
Gnostic*

To clarify this sense of inner dialogue, most
Gnostics spoke of a juxtaposition between the soul
and the ego. Daniel presented the individual's
aspects as follows:

*In these Gnostic teachings we have the ego,
and our soul or divine being. – Daniel, Gnostic*

Christians, like Gnostics, spoke of the need to
connect within, as Isabel would say:

*You need to be in contact with the spirit that
you have inside, your soul. – Isabel, Christian*

The distinction between the soul and other
entities of the same phenomenon were made clear.
James associated the concept of soul with the
concept of self. Specifically, the soul would be the
real self:

You've got the small self, which is completely conceptual and it's not there. Whereas the real self is beyond definition, it's because either has no attributes, or it's constantly changing. – James, Gnostic

Also atheists spoke of the duality of the self, although they did not make a clear distinction between the two parts. Ryan, in particular, spoke of self-reflections as a way to envision his own life:

I have plenty of moments of self-reflection in terms of how to lead the life I wanna lead, how do I get to the point where I want to get to in life. – Ryan, atheist

I-me-God

Firstly, for Christians, if there is a soul then there must be a God we are connected to. Rose clearly established this by saying that:

I would say that the soul is our religious concept so that if there is a thing it's a religious concept so therefore there's a connection to god. - Rose, Christian

Connecting with God means being connected within, as Christians explicitly discussed. For them, being in contact with God depends upon the maintenance of, and thus a connection with, one's own soul. Amelie explained that the individual has to ensure that their own soul is clean:

The more we try to cleanse our soul or maintain our soul, then, I think we are in a better condition to connect with God – Amelie, Christian

Eve revealed that being engaged in a relationship with God has an inner personal function for her, the possibility to self-reflect:

This relationship is about me exploring myself as well, if that makes sense. – Eve, Christian

More into the advantages that Christians sense out of their functional relationship with God, Oliver happily discussed the therapeutic effects for talking to God, or his soul, and having his life priorities refreshed in mind:

I can talk to him that I need to it and he helps me to establish whether it is that important or not. I would like to think that that's God or my soul reminding me of the important things in my life – Oliver, Christian

Gnostics set out the first step of a good life in the connection with God, the inner divine force. Stella advised that:

The first step is to connect with our inner being, or inner god, inner Christic energy and then the rest will come along.- Stella, Gnostic

Categories of belief

This theme departs slightly from giving a direct answer to the RQ. However, it serves to highlight the fuzzy differences between the categories of belief I used in this study. Most participants did not raise any issues with the affiliation to the category of belief they were interviewed for. However, amongst atheists, Mike completely dissociated from the category of belief he had originally chosen to be interviewed for. Similarly, Chloe partially rejected claims of supernaturalness in the Christian faith. Apart from Dylan, all Gnostics, on the other hand, while identifying with the principles of Gnosticism, tended to reject the label 'Gnostic' and made no reference to whether their Gnosticism was of some sort of Christian nature. Others set clear guidelines of what being a Christian, atheist, or Gnostic meant to them.

Christians

Amongst those who identified as Christians, the main underlying conviction was that their sense of being Christian corresponds to their internal struggle between human instincts, rationality, and respect for God. As Oliver confessed:

Being a Christian is a constant battle between your conscious thoughts and human desires and your respect for God, desire to honour a God as your creator. – Oliver, Christian

Some Christians were keen to draw a line and mark a distinction within the teachings of Christianity. This distinction was described as modern Christianity. Chloe explained this approach as follows:

For me and for modern day Christians, a Christian is someone who believes in the values of Christianity especially the values of loving one another, loving yourself. Jesus, nowadays, he's a prophet or somebody who had a different way of looking at things. I don't believe he was the son of God and that's why I don't believe there's this father figure that has sent through the virgin birth. I don't believe that anymore. – Chloe, Christian

Also, Christianity can be lived as a personal and intimate connection, not necessarily as a community experience. Eve frankly said:

For me, even though I'm Catholic, it's not so much attending church. I don't feel I have to attend church in order to have a relationship with God. For me it's more of a personal connection. So I pray quite regularly. But I wouldn't necessarily do that in front of other people. For me it's more of a personal and intimate relationship and connection that I have. – Eve, Christian

It was even more dramatic the contribution of Rose who identified as a Christian for bureaucratic purposes only, due to her social background:

I don't go to church, I don't pray, but if I have to fill in a form I'll still tick that I'm a catholic in that box. But I think it's more about where I grew up more so than anything. – Rose, Christian

Atheists

For all atheists apart from Mike and Penny, the characterising values of an atheist can be summarised as the rejection for explanations that transcend human capabilities:

Values in terms of atheism is just not believing in anything beyond the human, or beyond chance or coincidence as an explanation for why things happen. – Hazel, atheist

The main underlying motive for being atheists is the lack of factual evidence that could justify a spiritual side along a more material one. John put it this way:

I think probably to be an atheist you probably have pushed the spiritual side away. I like facts. I think most atheists are fact based. Where's the evidence? – John, atheist

Others, like Ryan, noted how their atheist identity relied upon religious concepts, probably as a way to show the coexistence of fundamentally different ideas that will never conciliate into a single view:

I would actually probably draw a lot of parallels with the religious world to present my overall personal values and then to present my own view of the world as an atheist. – Ryan, atheist

Yet, although remarking her atheist identity to affirm that she did not believe in the existence of God, Penny admitted to believe in spirituality and acknowledged that there is something beyond human understanding:

I feel I am sort of spiritual person but I don't believe there's like a God. I think like, I am an atheist obviously, but I do think I am a spiritual person and there's something there but I don't necessarily know what it is. – Penny, atheist

An incredible surprise was the unannounced self-revelation of Mike. Towards the end of his interview, he revealed he was not feeling being an atheist but a Gnostic.

I don't feel like I'm an atheist. I don't believe in any specific god which is defined by the current religions in this world. But atheists believe there's nothing, I believe there's something. I feel I'm a Gnostic. – Mike, atheist

Gnostics

All Gnostics spoke of the meaning of Gnosticism (Pagels, 1979). They all referred to the inner knowledge that can be gained to understand oneself as well as the world. For them, the meaning of being a Gnostic can be represented by James's words:

It's gaining knowledge from the inside because real knowledge, [...] knowledge of your states, your true identity is and how reality works for you only comes from the inside. – James, Gnostic

However, an important premise to understand the group identity of Gnostics is that no Gnostic person explicitly stated that they were Gnostics. Being a Gnostic, said with the words of Stella, is more about aspiring to Gnosticism, as a way to obtain the latent inner knowledge:

I haven't been considered myself to be a Gnostic but I do feel as an aspirant to gnosis, to Gnosticism. – Stella, Gnostic

Most of the Gnostic participants regarded Gnosticism as the path signed by Samael Aon Weor. However, David also explained that identifying oneself as a Gnostic would be just attaching oneself a label and, thus, being restricted within the paradigm of that particular set of ideas and notions:

Gnosis is a teaching that comes from Master Samael Aon Weor, we're talking about this Gnosis. This is new Gnosticism, in essence. I don't want to attach myself to any kind of label so I wouldn't like to call myself Gnostic or an esotericist or nything like that. – David, Gnostic

Like for the other categories, also the individual participants who follow Gnosticism tended to specify their own approach to the identity deriving from their own category of belief. Internal nuances, also in the case of Gnostics, kept trespassing the boundaries of their category to reach out other systems of beliefs. As a passing comment, Dylan wanted to clarify that Gnostics are actually Christians:

Gnostics are Christians by the way. – Dylan, Gnostic

Discussion

In this section I will discuss the findings obtained by the analysis of the interviews conducted with Christian, Atheist, and Gnostic participants. The discussion will aim to answer the following RQ:

How do Christians, Gnostics, and atheists make meaning of their subjective experience of God?

The findings seem to suggest that there are concepts rotating around the belief in supernatural agency that need to be considered for further discussion in the CSR. This will allow a comprehensive understanding of the relationship between subjective experience and belief in God.

The idea of God

Most participants spoke of a metaphysical and transcendental reality wherein everything is connected. In particular, Christians, Gnostics, and some atheists defined God as the omnipresent reality. This idea is consistent with Hart's (2013) description of God as the transcendental reality that eludes any limit and excludes any finite entity from one another, although it contains them without contradiction, in a holistic fashion (Aristotle, 1953). This notion is in neat contrast with the attempt of CSR's (Barrett, 1996) to assign God to any specific ontological category.

Furthermore, according to Christians and Gnostics, the individual is connected with this omnipresent reality through their soul which, they previously explained, represents the individual's consciousness. While this feeling finds its echo in Hart's (2013) idea that consciousness is the kernel of human experience, be it physical or metaphysical, there seems to be no indication by CSR's (Barrett and Keil, 2004; Boyer, 2001; Pyysiäinen, 2004) about the connection believers experience of their self with any wider transcendental reality.

The concept of soul

Consistent with the notion of "cause in esse" given by Hart (2013), most participants spoke of the soul or self as the core essence of the individual that envelops the qualities of the person; feelings, knowledge, and behaviours. This is in line with

Smart's (1996) observation that many ancient traditions associated the idea of the soul with what nowadays we call self. This can be explained by Leary and Buttermore's (2003) theory of the conceptual self; the ability to represent one's own experience in abstract and symbolic ways. In fact, participants showed their ability to conceptualise and represent through the symbol of soul, or self, their subjective experience of existence. Indeed, Harris (2014) notes that the psyche is simply an idea to illustrate the awareness the individual has of their own being. Awareness, or consciousness, is the substance whereby the individual self can make any sort of experience. That sense so distinctive that can be thought of as capable of outliving the corporeal body, also according to participants. In fact, in line with Pyysiäinen (2009), participants gave an account of the soul as the feeling of a force animating their bodies. Therefore, the concepts of soul and self are based upon the sense of a seemingly independent inner being that regulates the life of the individual.

Agency

In this study, all participants claimed to have agency against the idea that God could ever predetermine their life. Even believers spoke of the authorship of all of their actions, both conscious and unconscious. Unfortunately, there is not much literature in CSR that could help disentangle the relation between supernatural agency and one's own self-agency. The HADD evoked by CSR's (Barrett, 2004) only attempts to explain the belief in supernatural agents for events that take place externally to the individual.

However, participants also spoke of the soul as a force animating the body. This is in line with Hart's (2013) distinction between "cause in esse" and "cause in fiery". The "cause in fiery" or "cause in becoming" is that inner force that can have an impact on other things of the same kind. Also, participants spoke of free will in relation to God. In particular, Gnostics associated to a supernatural level the explicit sense of agency (Voyer and Franks, 2014) an individual can experience. This thought should motivate further discussion in CSR around cognitive mechanisms that could explain the subjective experience of supernatural agency.

Intersubjectivity

All participants spoke of their relationship with their self or soul as an intersubjective phenomenon where two or more subjects would be in a connection as seemingly autonomous selves (Reich, 2010). Against the assumption of atheists, Christians showed to be aware of the metaphorical consistence of their intersubjective phenomenon taking place between them and God. Indeed, both Christians and Gnostics based their relationships with God upon their inner intersubjectivity. In fact, consistently with the ideas of Leary and Buttermore (2003) and Luhmann (1990) regarding the sense of privateness and separateness that distinguishes the human individual, participants showed motivation in engaging with their God to overcome this issue. This is not reflected in the HUI device postulated by Pyysiäinen (2009). Nor this device accounts for the participants' feelings of being able to engage with their own soul. Again, this is the main recurrent issue of cognitive devices being postulated assuming that the meanings the individual produces are only to do with external phenomena. Rather, my findings suggest that the reasoning of Harris (2014) as well as Nichols (2000) in regards to a ToM working primarily to produce the individual's sense of self should be further discussed, also in relation to the belief in God, and obviously the soul. As the findings revealed, Christians and Gnostics highlighted the issue of interdependence between the inner self and God which, however, is not discussed in the relevant literature perused for this study. More attention should be devoted to the subject of interdependence in further research.

Categories of belief

The fact that some participants dissociated from the category of belief they had chosen to be interviewed for, and the general attitude of Gnostics to refuse any labelling, reflects Clements's (2016) criticism of social surveys for their over-simplification in putting people with different religious perspectives into the category of 'none'. A category (Berger, 2015) that literally includes a whole spectrum of people who does or does not believe in God; or people who identify completely, slightly, or not at all with any religious affiliation. Finally, the resulting fuzziness between categories is consistent with Woodhead's (2014) analysis of social surveys where she identifies as 'fuzzy nones' those who had been categorised as having no religion.

Limitations

The limitations of this study are mainly associated with the set up. The main limitation is related to the review of the topic guide. Reviewing the topic guide meant that some participants went through a different set of questions in their interviews. Nevertheless, this helped to improve my control for time availability, and give a new direction to the study. Indeed, dropping certain questions meant not being able to yield relevant data for the original RQ which was focused on the sense of self-agency in relation to supernatural agency. Although I am happy with the unexpected direction that the study took, it remains an opportunity for future studies to explore such relationship between self-agency and supernatural agency.

Conclusions

This study aimed to explore how people from three different categories of belief, namely Christians, atheists and Gnostics, make meaning of their subjective experience of God. The study originated from the current literature gap in CSR for what concerns the relation between subjective experience and supernatural experience. This study shows that people's accounts of their subjective experience can yield insights that could be useful to complement the theories already offered by CSR's. Specifically, people's feeling about their soul and its relationship with God could be of use to CSR to expand on the functionality of current cognitive devices that currently do not take people's feelings and intuitions into account. Indeed, findings indicate that it is fundamentally necessary to integrate the subjective experience of the individual to produce more comprehensive explanations of the belief in God, and go beyond theoretical assumptions.

Furthermore, talking of their subjective experience with God, participants undoubtedly suggested that their idea of God is an idea, if not *the one* idea, that shows the great achievements of human intellect. Formulating and comprehending such a highly transcendental concept that eludes the physical reality and envelops it at the same time, we are meant to elevate the human to a level of experience that goes beyond the boundaries of ontological categories. "*If you comprehend it, it is not God*" (Augustine, Sermon 52, 16): yet, it might not be as Augustine said if we can comprehend God through the 'I' of the soul.

APPENDICES

Appendix 1 – Demographics

Pseudonym	Gender
Christians	*F: 6; M: 1*
Emma	F
Isabel	F
Oliver	M
Charlotte	F
Amelie	F
Eve	F
Chloe	F
Atheists	*F: 3; M: 4*
Penny	F
Hazel	F
John	M
Mike	M
Jack	M
Ryan	M
Ely	F
Gnostics	*F: 1; M: 6*
James	M
Jacob	M
Daniel	M
David	M
Gabriel	M
Dylan	M
Stella	F

Appendix 2 - Sample interview

Interviewer: Thank you very much for accepting to be interviewed for my research study. I will start by asking you how long have you been an atheist for?

Penny: Probably about since I was 15, 16. 15 or years now.

Interviewer: What made you decide to become an atheist?

Penny: I was a Christian. I wasn't brought up a Christian but I had friends that were Christians and used to go to their house after school. And then I got really disillusioned with the church because I just found that what they were telling us wasn't very credible. I felt quite manipulated by the church. It was like an evangelical Christian thing and was all a bit intense. And then I just probably I got a bit wiser and then I decided I wasn't really believing much of what they were saying anymore. So I left that.

Interviewer: So you said you weren't born as a Christian. Is that correct?

Penny: As in my family didn't raise me in a religious household, no. My dad was religious when he was a similar age and he was quite involved in church as well, but then he turned away from it. Just a bit older than I was. So he had been there already but not when I was alive. And my mum's dad is a scientist so they're all, and that side of the family is very atheist.

Interviewer: How would you describe being an atheist?

Penny: Just not believing in God.

Interviewer: Ok. Would you admit the existence of any other supernatural entity?

Penny: I feel I am sort of spiritual person but I don't believe there's like... I think it's like beyond our capabilities of understanding.

Interviewer: What do you mean by that?

Penny: I don't know what it is but there may be something but I don't think we...I don't know.

Interviewer: So how would describe your principles as an atheist?

Penny: I would say I believe that there may be something after death but I don't believe in heaven and hell and I don't believe there's a god and I don't believe in bible stories as I think they are human interpretations like they're moral stories. And I just believe in being a good person. I know right from wrong and I feel don't need religion that constantly tells me what to do. That's pure consciousness.

Interviewer: What do you know about entities like God, angels, and demons?

Penny: I don't know.

Interviewer: You said you don't believe in God and other supernatural entities. But you said there may be something after death. Do you mind expanding on that?

Penny: Yes. I believe that there's somewhere else that we go and I don't believe in ghosts. So I don't really know what it would be that we go after death. But I find it quite hard also to believe that we just go in ground and then we become carbon because that's quite hard for a human to really accept because you then you do have just one life which I do believe like we are here we have a short life and we should live it. You know it's no point in believing it thinking there's something afterwards because I think this is it. I also struggle to think that you then just cease to exist because it's quite hard to comprehend.

Interviewer: Would you believe in a person's soul?

Penny: Yes. I think so

Interviewer: How would you describe a person's soul?

Penny: Like the thing that is inside you that is kind of like sort of who you are, like your feelings maybe? Your consciousness maybe? Like voice in your head kind of talking to you

Interviewer: Can you tell me about a time when you felt really engrossed in what you were doing?

Penny: Writing. When I was writing my novel I would have days where I would sit down and just write and I was completely engrossed in it. Nothing else was really happening.

Interviewer: What were your feelings?

Penny: Amazing. It feels amazing and like a sort of I always think it feels not really me, like it comes from somewhere higher up and I'm sort of like a vessel for some sort of higher creative flow that's happening.

Interviewer: How did you feel about control over your actions and thoughts in those moments?

Penny: I felt more like it just sort of happens with the writing. When I write something I can't explain... if I go back and someone says how did you do that? I find it difficult to explain it. Or if there is metaphors in there, that I know it's my consciousness and my unconscious working together but this unconscious things happening and I'm putting these metaphors in and then I look back and it's really f* clever. But I wasn't consciously trying to be clever. So I find it hard, I don't really think there is much control. I know there is me doing it but I don't think, I m sitting there thinking how am I gonna construct this sentence? When you've got that flow, it just happens. I think that's when you create your best.

Interviewer: How do you think a believer would describe such a feeling and situation?

Penny: They're probably believe it's kind of God working through you maybe? Which I can kind of understand because it's a spiritual thing does feel like there is something else. They would probably believe they're doing God's work. But I don't think it's like that because the stuff I write is so dark, and I can't think is like God. Not really.

Interviewer: So are you saying that because it's dark you can't believe it's God?

Penny: I don't know if God would be into probably for some of the stuff I write.

Interviewer: Would you associate God with anything?

Penny: Yes, like the clouds and holy. I do feel like it's something else like a creative force. I think there is something like a creative energy or that's not does not God. Or maybe it's just a perception of it.

Interviewer: Anytime you ever felt you were doing something you didn't want to do?

Penny: Being at work.

Interviewer: Do you have any example of a particular action or task that you didn't enjoy doing?

Penny: When I first started doing [Task omitted for confidentiality] and I had to do loads in one go. It felt like really this is against what you should be doing. And this made me physically hurt my neck. Really weird. When I started doing it I felt really unconformable.

Interviewer: What motivated you, then?

Penny: I was doing it to keep my job and my wage. If I could do anything like writing all day, but I can't pay my bills.

Interviewer: Can you tell me of an instance where you couldn't control your thoughts?

Penny: Yes when I have anxiety I have difficulty to control my thoughts. I feel really anxious and is not really rationale. So I have trouble to make … my rationale part seems to leave my thought process. So I have trouble control my thoughts if they're kind of negative, and I feel stressed out.

Interviewer: How do you think a believer would understand a similar situation?

Penny: Probably, that they felt far away from God. Or maybe they don't feel it so much if they have a strong faith they would just think oh God will be there.

Interviewer: So you say that if they feel anxious they may think they have a disconnection with their God, from their faith. Is it what you just said?

Penny: And they were not in tune. But I guess it was similar because in those moments I would feel disconnected from things. When I'm in the flow writing I'm not anxious at all. It's kind of the opposite, I feel disconnected from the universe I guess where I get all the creative flow and energy

Interviewer: So are you saying you were feeling anxious because of that sense of disconnection with things?

Penny: Yes. Maybe.

Interviewer: How would you describe unconscious desires in relation to your atheistic values?

Penny: What do you mean? Things I'm not aware of?

Interviewer: Yes.

Penny: Can you give me an example? Or actually maybe it's best we skip this question?

Interviewer: Sure, yes. No problem. Can you tell me about a time when you found yourself daydreaming?

Penny: I daydream quite a lot. Like when I'm bored or when I'm walking. I used to make up stories in my head just stuff. Like kind of other characters.

Interviewer: Any example?

Penny: I daydream about things I want to happen. I used to daydream a lot about my speech and my book launch. Like there was a million people there. Like when I will be famous. In the shower as well, a lot of the time. In the shower I kind of daydream a lot that sort of things.

Interviewer: *When you daydream, do you feel having any control over your actions and thoughts?*

Penny: I think so, yeah. I'm not really thinking what I was doing. so if I'm walking I'm just so going, I'm not really in a different place of my daydream. I'm not really in reality. I'm in the daydream but I'm still walking without falling over obviously. But it's like I'm not thinking about that, I'm just moving.

Interviewer: *So you keep walking without thinking about walking?*

Penny: Yeah.

Interviewer: *And you think you can control your thoughts when you daydream?*

Penny: Yes, I think so. Sometimes, with daydream you let yourself go off and like kind of spiral off, I think you can control... I think you're in control.

Interviewer: Ok

Penny: It's hard. Because when you are in a daydream you are not necessarily or never think of a consciously on daydreaming. I never thought oh what I do I daydream. it's just happens

Interviewer: So are you saying it is something that just happens to you?

Penny: Yeah, you don't sit down and say can I daydream now? My mind wonders off when someone is talking and is boring or whatever. My brain is something like [inaudible] and goes off on its own

Interviewer: How do you feel a believer would interpret that?

Penny: I don't know. I don't think they would think that that was something to do with God. I was just thinking when I was like a Christian if I thought I was different.

Interviewer: So are you saying that a believer wouldn't associate it with God or anything to do with it?

Penny: Maybe if they are dreaming about... because I'm thinking maybe they would think that dreams were like from God and that is the same thing but you just awake and still be your unconscious. They may think it's something to do with God.

Interviewer: What do you think about dreams instead?

Penny: Dreams are weird. I had a really good dream. Amazing. I think it was last night or the night before. You know when it's like a film, like there s a script and I woke up and I'm oh my God, that's my next book. Then obviously is not it's like shit... (laughter) there are so many plot holes... And sometimes I think why don't I come up with things like that when it's a daydream? So I can like, I don't know, when you have a dream you kind of forget. I tend to forget most of it, very quickly. I think dreams are weird because something has triggered what you're dreaming out but I can never work it out because sometimes is so abstract and I would think about obviously I've seen something and something has fed in and I haven't consciously picked up on it but then it's there and I'm thinking about it. They're so weird! Really f* weird.

Interviewer: Have you ever had dreams where you felt in control?

Penny: Yeah, lucid dreaming... I don't know how much I wanna say about my lucid dreaming

Interviewer: Ok...

Penny: It's great.

Interviewer: How do you think a believer would understand a lucid dream?

Penny: I don't know if they would think it's like they would be connected with God or not. I use lucid dreams when if I wake up and then you drift in and out of your sleep and its always like in the morning when I wake up and dozing I use lucid dreams. I guess as a lot of people fly. People with faith would think maybe oh look I'm an angel. Lucid dreams are really weird as well. I don't understand them.

Interviewer: What do you think is the role of God and angels and devils for a believer when they interpret their dreams?

Penny: If they dream about an angel?

Interviewer: Even if they don't...

Penny: If an angel were in their dream they would most people with faith would think that that was a message from God, I think. Even if it wasn't so black and white, if there was something in their dreams that they could interpret like that. When I was a church, we used to go on about dreams and what people dreamt about... but then I think it s a bit selective, because if maybe the devil showed up in their dreams I don't know if they would, I was thinking maybe you can be selective and you can choose anything to be a message if you want. Loads of people want to have a certain message and you can find it in being told to you if you're looking enough for it. Sometimes it's a very clear message, even if you don't want that message you can receive it. But things like dreams can be interpreted like, I think it is really subjective in the way they can be interpreted and in different ways. I'm sure some people with faith could interpret a dream to mean something that they want it to mean and they can back up what they want to ... oh God is [*inaudible*] is ... cause he's told me this in a dream and so I'm going to buy a Ferrari because it's ok.

Interviewer: How would you describe the relationship between free will and the idea of God?

Penny: Say it again?

Interviewer: How would you describe the relationship between free will and the idea of God? do you think there is anything that differentiates them or can they be the same thing?

Penny: Humans have free will... I don't know. Let me come back to the question..

Interviewer: While religious people pray or meditate, you as an atheist, have any practice or ritual you engage in at any time?

Penny: No but I do meditate and I think its good for your mind. It's relaxing, but apart from that, no. I don't think so.

Interviewer: How does it relaxes you?

Penny: By clearing your mind. If I do it in the morning, it makes me focus on what is important. So if I wake up same if I do the morning pages. I write six pages when I wake up and I used to do it and even if you wake up and feel depressed and whatever if you write you kind of gets the stuff out of you like a therapist. And it just helps me to start the day in the right frame of mind. And it reminds me of what's important what is really like the little things that stress you over and that are not really important. Just makes me feel more focused.

Interviewer: Ok. How would you describe your feelings of control over your thoughts while you meditate?

Penny: I find it quite difficult to control my thoughts. I find that clear my mind is very difficult here, 'cause you are meant to do this things where if you have a thought you acknowledge that you have a thought and then you put it away and then just carry on. Just but I find it really difficult for a thought not to creep in to my brain.

Interviewer: Sorry, I'm not clear. When you meditate, do you try to concentrate or you try to clear your mind of every thought?

Penny: Yeah, clearing your mind, but because I'm not very good at it and I haven't done it for a long time, I concentrate on like a kind of app that tells me scan down your body, you see something to concentrate on something which isn't your thoughts. And then visualizations, think about there been a bowl of light there in your heart that then expands. So you see you're asked to concentrate on something and trying not to think like, my God I'm really late, or I'm hungry. Like the annoying other thoughts.

Interviewer: So are you talking about a guided meditation? And have you ever done any non-guided meditation?

Penny: Yeah, but not as much, I find it quite hard. I guess it depends if I feel like, like if I have a lot going on and I'm stressed and I was like always running late, I would find it very hard just to sit down and unguided meditation but if I was on the beach in Goah and everything was chilled, it would probably be easier. So just more relaxed already.

Interviewer: Have you ever done any group meditation?

Penny: No.

Interviewer: Do you think there would be any difference?

Penny: At the end of yoga yeah. We'd do a little meditation bit, I don't know if that counts. I don't think there is any difference because I just, even when I do yoga, I just am very like concentrated on like … what people are doing. I just focus on myself.

So when I'm meditating and my eyes are already closed I don't think there is any difference, really.

Interviewer: Ok. Have you ever felt a link between your own actions and something bigger and deeper than just yourself?

Penny: Yeah! Well, like the a karma.

Interviewer: How would you describe the concept of karma?

Penny: If you're good to people and friendly and you smile, its gonna make other people, like they're gonna react to your energy with positive energy cause that's what you're putting out, I don't think there's anything like weird or spiritual. I think it's pretty basic and like almost scientific. Like if I do something nice or I'm nice to be around or I smile or whatever you're probably going to be nice to other people. Like when I'm mean at work to you I feel like I shouldn't do that and then I feel you'll probably, you wouldn't be mean, but probably you don't wanna talk to like ... it's not black and white... if everyone was "oh I can't deal with my work and... everyone would be sad".

Interviewer: So, are you talking about connections with other people?

Penny: Yeah, but I'm not sure, yeah I still think you should do... if you pick a lizard off the street I would still think that... I just think if I do it more people are going to do it as well.

Interviewer: And where does it take us if everyone does it?

Penny: To a better world?

Interviewer: So are you saying your actions are connected with this bigger thing than just you?

Penny: Yeah. Like the oneness. Which I do quite feel like that. I feel like that even more since I've been doing meditation, I feel more connected to everyone. Because I didn't really feel that before. And I didn't feel like that when I was a Christian. I don't know if that's a religious thing or not. I definitely think that it just came out of meditation and yoga. A feeling that everyone is connected.

Interviewer: You said a word: oneness?

Penny: Yeah

Interviewer: Would you expand a bit on that, please?

Penny: I feel that we're just like that we're all... that everyone is having their human experience but were all kind of the same and connected, like I was saying, if I'm nice to you you're experience is gonna be nicer and the energy is gonna be better. I would find it very difficult to describe like it feels but I definitely feel something. Yeah, it's like a feeling of oneness.

Interviewer: Ok   Have you ever had a religious experience?

Penny: Yeah. The Holy Spirit.

Interviewer: Can you please expand a bit more on this, please?

Penny: The church I used to go to, as it was like evangelical. So they had, they were very big on the Holy Spirit, so there were people speaking in tongues, people falling over, like ... I don't really know how to describe it but I was like uncontrollably laughing and then uncontrollably out crying. Like so emotional. But I put it down to, now, that I'm thinking about, it's like the energy and I was also a teenager, and I think I was kind of easily manipulated at that age and I definitely been pushed over as well when a guy said "the power of the Holy Spirit is in you" and I have pushed over. I think that's not ok.

Interviewer: He pushed you physically, you mean?

Penny: Yeah physically pushed over. They obviously want to show that the Holy Spirit is there. Its that sort of things that lead me not to believe in it. Because I just thought is down to music and its so very manipulative. It does make you emotional and there are lots of people there who are struggling and, I'm not saying this is why, but there are lots of weak people. People who are trying to fill a hole in their life with religion, which is fine but they get together and in that church it would be just that crazy and then people get drunk on the Holy Spirit.

Interviewer: Have you ever had a genuine religious experience?

Penny: I thought that was genuine because I find it hard to explain it without there being no God. Why is so emotional suddenly, and the speaking in tongue I find it quite difficult to explain because it's weird.

Interviewer: Do you mean people could speak other languages?

Penny: They could speak other languages. I think the human brain is weird and I just think I was very emotional. And I am very emotional when I listen to music anyway. So with a lot of people around with that kind same sort of thing you kind of want to have that experience? You want to be laughing or crying or whatever. I think it's not a genuine experience but at the time I thought it was. And I can see why people do think it is. And I've never spoken in tongues only heard people doing it. So I don't know how it feels like so maybe they're just making it up a language or I don't know. But I feel like I had a spiritual experiences when I've been travelling or with the writing a lot where you just feel very happy and the oneness. I don't know. That's not really a religious experience. I would say, I describe that as a religious experience. Because spiritual is when...

Interviewer: *You feel connected again...*

Penny: Yeah yeah...

Interviewer: *And do you think is one of those experiences that you can create and re-create at will, anytime you wanted?*

Penny: No, I think... well. I can go up a mountain at sunrise and see something amazing and there's a bigger chance that I'll have a spiritual experience than sitting at the LSE doing transcripts emails. But I don't think that I would ever go that mountain and have a religious experience. It's like worse than that. It comes to you and sometimes is so like unexpected. And you have that feeling I don't think you can create it at will. No, you can go to places that I'm likely I would never think that you can make it happen.

Interviewer: Ok. So, what do you think is the main difference between the human normal day to day experience and a spiritual or religious experience like the one you've just described.

Penny: It's very hard to describe it. I feel like a lot of the time in your normal experience you're on auto-pilot. You see it's not really like the same, you walk you breath, you don't think about that kind of thing. A lot of the time stuff I do at work I can kind of switch my brain off and just do it or whatever, but when I had these spiritual experiences I feel very aware of where I am and my place and time.

Interviewer: Ok. So you said that spiritual experiences come to you. How do you think a believer would interpret that?

Penny: Yeah. They would think that that was something from God, I guess. Or like a reassurance that God is there and loves them, probably.

Interviewer: So, after you had your spiritual experiences have you ever felt something has changed within yourself?

Penny: Yes, I think. I felt kind of I got to know myself a bit better or I've learnt something about myself or, yeah, I think it does. It's hard to pinpoint what it is. But not every experience...

Interviewer: Not every religious or spiritual experience, are you referring to that?

Penny: Yes, but I think lots of them make you feel more connected.

Interviewer: Ok. Going back to a previous question, let's see if I can reformulate that: how do you understand what is God, at least for a believer?

Penny: For a believer it's a, I guess probably it varies but for Christians that I used to know God is like their comforter and like obviously when they pray they can speak to him. It's like it gives people hope. I get it as it's really hard to be in the world and that's why I say I find it really difficult to think that we can't just be in a grave and that's it because it's really hard when you realise you're basically on your own. Even if you have connections with other humans, at the end of the day it's just you on your own. You're gonna die on your own, and you'll never really, and i don't think ever really gonna be able to understand someone else's mind even if you are super close to them, your partner for like 20 years or something. He's still a different person to you. So I think, it's really that lonely thought, if you really think about it, that's why lots of people do so many things to be with other people and don't be on their own. So I get why it would be comforting to have a god or believe in something that is bigger than you, that you don't have to worry. Yeah, if you're just a good person, at the end of the day you'll go to heaven. And if any shit happen you can just be like have some sort of comfort that there's some bigger plan, so that when unfair stuff happens and I think it would give people hope that there's a reason and a meaning. And it's not just everything's chaos and bad luck basically. Even if shit things happen that's hard to deal with. And like chaos theory, I think just its just something people hold on to give them meaning in their life: meaning and comfort.

Interviewer: And how does affect free will and free choice for those who believe in it?

Penny: What do you mean those who believe in it?

Interviewer: Do you think that those who believe in God have their free will affected by this?

Penny: So you mean if whatever they do there's already a path?

Interviewer: Yeah. Do you think whether their free will is constrained or elicited?

Penny: Yeah. When I was in Cambodia, I stayed in a Christian household because it was kind of missionary. English people there are mission people. They did the work I was doing, so really anyone was just doing it because, no I'm sure they were doing the same I was doing. Obviously I think that sometimes Christians do it if that wins with God or whatever. And this girl she like she rode a bike she rode it very dangerously. She had a son as well. She was like my age. Riding her motorbike and she was like "if I crash and die it'll be what God wants". And I was thinking that's so stupid. I met lots of people like that that "oh well if this happens: If I cross the road and get hit by a bus, it was God's will." That's really dumm! I think.

You're just passing the buck of making any decision in your life because you just think, oh, well, like if your job fucks up, or ruin a relationship and you can just be, well, this is my path, this is what... yeah, I just think it's passing the buck. It's not. You're not owning your own destiny. Which I think you should. You're gonna make your own decisions and, yeah, everyone makes mistakes, everyone makes some pretty bad horrific mistakes that change their whole life and you have just to live with that. People can't think so they say they it has pre-written for them which I don't believe at all.

Interviewer: Ok.

Penny: Is that fine?

Interviewer: Absolutely fine. Do you think there is anything you want to add in regards to what we talked to day? Anything you'd like to expand more?

Penny: No. I still can't think about the unconscious. But I'll think about that because it's just such an interesting question...

Interviewer: Well, if anytime it comes up to your mind and you would like to share, I'll be pleased to add it on to your interview.

Penny: I think like, I am an atheist obviously, but I do think I am a spiritual person and there's something there but I don't necessarily know what it is. Obviously I cannot explain it very well. But definitely there's something. I think through meditation and yoga they made me more spiritual person. So there's definitely something in there but I don't think there's something that is disconnected from us that's ruling over I think. Its within you I think. Even when you look pass on your mind, when you're like on mushrooms and stuff you go to different places: that's spiritual experience. A lot people say that it's like: it's what Christians would say, it's like a God experience. It's in your mind.

Interviewer: So if you had to summarise the definition of spiritual for a lay person or a child?

Penny: An experience you can have internally. It's too hard.

Interviewer: Excellent! Thank you ever so much for your time and for the great insights you offered.

References

Aristotle. (1957). *De Anima. On the Soul.* Translated by W. S. Hett. Loeb Classical Library, 288. London: Heinemann.

Auerbach, J.S. (1998). Dualism, Self-Reflexivity, and Intersubjectivity Commentary on Paper by Sheldon Bach, *Psychoanalytic Dialogues*, 8:5, 675-683, DOI: 10.1080/10481889809539282

Barrett, J.L. (2004). *Why Would Anyone Believe in God?* Lanham: Alta Mira Press.

Barrett, J.L. (2008). Coding and Quantifying Counterintuitiveness: Theoretical and Methodological Reflections. *Method and theory in the study of religion* 20(4), 308–38. DOI: 10.1163/157006808X371806

Barrett, J.L., & Keil, F.C. (1996). Conceptualizing a Nonnatural Entity: Anthropomorphism in God Concepts. *Cognitive Psychology* 31, 219-247 (1996) Article No. 0017. DOI: 10.1006/cogp.1996.0017

Bauer, M.W., & Gaskell, G. (2008). *Qualitative Researching with Text, Image and Sound. A Practical Handbook*. London: Sage Publication.

BBC. (2009-08-14). *Religions*. Retrieved from http://www.bbc.co.uk/religion/religions/christianity/beliefs/basics_1.shtml)

Berger, P. L. (2015). The *"Nones" and the "Buts"*. *The American Interest*. Retrieved from: https://www.the-american-interest.com/2015/05/06/the-nones-and-the-buts/

Boyatzis, R. (1998). *Transforming Qualitative Information: Thematic Analysis and Code Development*. Thousand Oaks, CA: Sage.

Boyer, P. (1994). *The Naturalness of Religious Ideas: a Cognitive Theory of Religion*. Berkley: University of California Press.

Boyer, P. (2000). Functional Origins of Religious Concepts: Ontological and Strategic Selection in Evolved Minds. *The Journal of the Royal Anthropological Institute*, 6(2), 195-214. Retrieved from http://www.jstor.org/stable/2660892

Boyer, P. (2001). *Religion Explained: The Human Instincts that Fashion Gods, Spirits, and Ancestors.* London: Vintage.

Braun, V., & Clarke, V. (2006). Using thematic analysis in psychology. *Qualitative research in psychology, 3 (2),* 77-101. Retrieved from: http://eprints.uwe.ac.uk/11735/2/thematic_analysis_r evised_-final.pdf.%20Accessed%202%20Oct%202017

Clements, B. (2016). Who are the 'religious nones' in Britain? Atheists, Agnostics or Something Else? Religion and the Public Sphere (26 Jul 2016). Blog. Retrieved from: http://eprints.lse.ac.uk/76494/

Collins Dictionary. (2018-08-05). *Soul.* Retrieved from https://www.collinsdictionary.com/dictionary/english/soul

Collins Dictionary. (2018-07-25). *Atheist.* Retrieved from https://www.collinsdictionary.com/dictionary/english/atheist

Dawkins, R. (2006). *The God Delusion.* London: Transworld Publishers.

Fereday, J., & Muir-Cochrane, E. (2006). Demonstrating Rigor Using Thematic Analysis: a Hybrid Approach of Inductive and Deductive Coding and Theme Development. *International Journal of Qualitative Methods* 2006, 5(1). https://doi.org/10.1177/160940690600500107

Fujii, L. A. (2012). Research Ethics 101: Dilemmas and Responsibilities. *PS: Political Science & Politics, 2012, Vol.45(4),* 717-723. DOI: 10.1017/S1049096512000819

Fylan F. (2005). Chapter 6: Semi-Structured Interviewing. In J. Miles, & P. Gilbert (Eds.), *A handbook of research methods for clinical and health psychology.* New York, USA: Oxford University Press.

Geden, A. S. (1922). *Comparative Religion.* London: Society for Promoting Christian Knowledge.

Gergely, G., & Csibra, G. (2003). Teleological Reasoning in Infancy: the Naïve Theory of Rational Action. *Trends in Cognitive Sciences* 7:287-92. http://citeseerx.ist.psu.edu/viewdoc/download?doi=1 0.1.1.331.5767&rep=rep1&type=pdf

Gray, J. (2018). *Seven Types of Atheism*. Milton Keynes: Allen Lane.

Guillemin, M., & Gillam, L. (2004). Ethics, Reflexivity, and "Ethically Important Moments" in Research. *Qualitative Inquiry, 2004, Vol.10(2),*261-280. DOI: 10.1177/1077800403262360

Harris, S. (2014). *Waking Up. Searching for Spirituality Without Religion*. London: Transworld Publishers.

Hart, D. B. (2013). *The Experience of God. Being, Consciousness, Bliss*. New Haven and London: Yale University Press.

Hitchens, C. (2007). *God is not Great*. London: Atlantic Books.

Hoeller, S. A. (1982). *The Gnostic Jung and the Seven Sermons to the Dead*. Wheaton, USA: Quest Books, Theosophical Publishing House

Hoeller, A. S. (2002). *Gnosticism. New Light on the Ancient Tradition of the Inner Knowing*. Wheaton, Illinois: Quest Books.

Jeannerod, M. (2003). The Mechanism of Self-Recognition in Human. *Behavioral Brain Research*, 142, 1-15. Retrieved from https://www.ncbi.nlm.nih.gov/pubmed/12798261

Keller, T. (2008). *The Reason for God. Belief in an Age of Scepticism*. London: Hodder & Stoughton.

Leary, M. R., & Buttermore, N. R. (2003). The Evolution of the Human Self: Tracing the Natural History of Self-Awareness. *Journal for the Theory of Social Behaviour*, December 2003, Vol.33(4), pp.365-404. DOI: 10.1046/j.1468-5914.2003.00223.x

Mayan, M. (2009). *Essentials of Qualitative Inquiry*. London: Routledge.

Mead, G. H. (1934, 2015). *Mind, Self, and Society*. London: The University Chicago Press.

Neisser, U. (1988). Five Kinds of Self-Knowledge. *Philosophical Psychology* 1 (1):35 – 59. doi.org/10.1080/09515088808572924

Nichols, S. (2000). The Mind's "I" and the Theory of Mind's "I": Introspection and Two Concepts of

Self. *Philosophical Topics,* 28(2), 171-199. Retrieved from http://www.jstor.org/stable/43154686

Nichols, S., & Stich, S.P. (2003). *Mindreading: an Integrated Account of Pretence, Self-Awareness, and Understanding Other Minds.* Oxford: Oxford University Press.

Pagels, E. (1979). *The Gnostic Gospels.* London: Phoenix.

Pew Research Centre. (December 19, 2012). *Global Attitudes & Trends.* Retrieved from: http://www.pewglobal.org/2012/12/20/slideshow-pew-researchs-global-year-in-review/pg_12-18-12_yearslides_00_title-2/

Pew Research Centre. (December 19, 2011). *Table: Christian Population in Numbers by Country.* Retrieved from: http://www.pewforum.org/2011/12/19/table-christian-population-in-numbers-by-country/

Pietkiewicz, I., & Smith, J. (2014). A Practical Guide to Using Interpretative Phenomenological. Analysis in Qualitative Research Psychology. *Psychological Journal,* 20, 1, 2014, 7-14. DOI: 10.14691/CPPJ.20.1.7

Pyysiäinen, I. (2004). Intuitive and Explicit in Religious Thought. *Journal of Cognition and Culture* 4(1), 123–50. DOI: 10.1163/156853704323074787

Pyysiäinen, I. (2009). *Supernatural Agents. Why We Believe in Souls, Gods, and Buddhas*. Oxford: University Press.

Reich, W. (2010). Three Problems of Intersubjectivity—And One Solution. *Sociological Theory*, 28(1), 40-63. Retrieved from http://www.jstor.org/stable/25746213

Rice, P. L., & Ezzy, D. (1999). *Qualitative Research Methods: a Health Focus*. South Melbourne (Australia): Oxford University Press.

Sicdic. [Sicdic]. (2014, Mar 11). *Quote Carl Jung I know God exists* [Video File]. Retrieved from: https://www.youtube.com/watch?v=HdpVosChMDc

Smart, N. (1996). *Dimensions of the Sacred. An Anatomy of the World's Beliefs*. London: Harper Collins Publishers.

Spencer, H. (1876). *The Principles of Sociology*. London: Williams & Norgate.

Tylor, E. B. (1958). *Religion in Primitive Culture.* New York: Harper & Row.

UK Data Service. (2018a). *Semi-Structured Interviews.* Retrieved March 25, 2018, from https://www.ukdataservice.ac.uk/teaching-resources/interview/semi-structured

UK Data Service. (2018b). *Consent for Data Sharing.* Retrieved March 25, 2018, from https://www.ukdataservice.ac.uk/manage-data/legal-ethical/consent-data-sharing

Voyer, B. & Franks, B. (2014). Toward a Better Understanding of Self-Construal Theory: An Agency View of the Processes of Self-Construal. *Review of General Psychology, 2014, Vol.18(2),* 101-114. DOI: 10.1037/gpr0000003

Woodhead, L. (2014). Launch Series: The 'Fuzzy' Nones. Non-religion and Secularity. Retrieved August 5, 2018 from: https://blog.nsrn.net/2014/03/07/launch-series-the-fuzzy-nones/

If you would like to put your feedback forward,
or discuss this study, please contact:

s.ridino@yahoo.com